The Clifton Poet and his Daughter Mattie (now deceased).

HEART MELODIES:
FOR STORM AND SUNSHINE.

FROM CLIFTONIA THE BEAUTIFUL.

By P. GABBITASS, the Clifton Poet,

ONCE A CARPENTER BOY.

Author of Select Poems, graciously accepted by Her Majesty the Queen, their
Royal Highnesses the Prince and Princess of Wales, Duke of Edinburgh,
late Duke of Albany, &c., &c.

CLIFTONIA THE BEAUTIFUL.

Yes, thou art beautiful !   Thy sylvan ridge,
And Avon wide, with grand Suspension Bridge,
From old St. Vincent's rocks I scan with glee,
And all have pure entrancing charms for me.

1885.

BRISTOL, CLIFTON, AND THROUGH ALL BOOKSELLERS.

Dedication.

TO

WILLIAM BUTLER, ESQ.,

OF CLIFTON GROVE,

A LONG-TRIED, TREASURED FRIEND, IN THE STORM AND SUNSHINE,

THIS VOLUME OF POEMS, PENNED UNDER VARIED CONDITIONS OF

LIFE, IS AFFECTIONATELY INSCRIBED BY THE WRITER.

Clifton, 1885.

THE hand that finds us in the storm,
  We grasp with joy amid the waves :
And feeling it are not forlorn,
  Because it is the hand that saves.

All grateful hearts will own that hand—
  When sunshine comes in varied form—
That brought their drifting barque to land,
  Despite the pelting of the storm.

CONTENTS.

CONTENTS—*Continued.*

CONTENTS—*Continued.*

Preface.

TO write one's own history is not an easy matter, and to do it faithfully may not always be a pleasant duty : nevertheless, if it be not so written, it had better not be penned at all—and, further, if no useful purpose be served by its production, it might well remain in oblivion. In this brief introduction to my strange life-history, I wish it to be understood that it is written at the urgent request of a dear daughter, now deceased. "You must write your own history, father," she said ; " it has been so varied, your experiences may be of use to many when you are gathered Home." If such should be the case, I shall be amply repaid for my toil. In it I shall endeavour to relate what I know *is true*, and more especially those scenes and circumstances relating to my pursuing the rough track, which for the last eleven years I have been walking in—the POET'S PATH : a path I never sought, and one in which I have had to do violence to my own feelings, many times, to tread. Nevertheless, I certainly believe it was one marked out for me by Providence : and, believing this, I have pursued it in the storm and sunshine ; and whatever may be found in this Volume of Poems to be useful in helping mankind to better life, will give me incessant joy while I live. But let them give all the glory to Another, Whose I am, and Whom I serve : remembering that the Treasure was placed in an earthen vessel, that the excellency of the power might be of God and not of man : for it is by His Grace alone that I am what I am, and that grace He has bestowed upon me, I trust, has not been given in vain.

Clifton, 1885. P. GABBITASS.

THE POET'S AUTOBIOGRAPHY.

E was born at Worksop, in the county of Nottingham: a pretty little market town, near the Dukeries of Welbeck and Clumber, and noted for its timber trade, and manufactories for Windsor chairs. His father for a number of years carried on a successful business in this department, which, after his decease, was conducted by his widow until their four children, then living, were brought up to man and womanhood.

The time the subject of this sketch was ushered into being, was one cold December night in the year 1822. He was born, I presume, much after the same manner as other babies, only he was,

Of course, their first-born baby boy—
His father's hope, and mother's joy !

and 'tis said there was a little extra rejoicing on that account. It is authoritatively stated that, on the occasion of his christening, there was quite a dispute as to what name he should bear: some of his friends wished him to be named after his mother's relatives, others declared he should be named after friends on his father's side ; and there is no knowing where the matter would have ended, had not his father, as a third party, stepped in and settled the matter in his own peculiar way. He told the varied disputants that the baby boy should not be named after any of their relatives, but after good old Peter Godfrey, a man in their employ : and he hoped that their little one would grow up like him. That is the reason the Clifton Poet bears the name of Peter, and as truth is sometimes stranger than fiction, so it is here: for good old Peter Godfrey was a poet, and of no mean order—for it is said that, through the public press, for weeks he had the mastery of a reverend gentleman, in a poetical discussion on Water Baptism. Of the Clifton Poet's ancestors it is not needful to say much. His mother's parents, whose name was Foster, occupied a farm near Womersly, in Yorkshire : where was born one of the best of mothers to her children in the wide, wide world ; and who, at the ripe age of eighty-four, in the year 1884, at Worksop, calmly passed away to rest. His grandsire on his father's side was a carpenter, and for many years worked at the bench for the Poet's father (he has given some sketches of both his grandsires in this book, in a poem entitled " Grandsires"). His great grandsire, Robert Gabbitass, was the Town Crier and Watchman at East Retford, and where, in gold lace uniform and three-cornered hat, he used to parade the streets and announce the passing hours of night—beside this he filled the post of assistant sheriff's officer, and once had the unpleasant duty of arresting at Newstead Abbey, in bed, the world-renowned poet, Lord Byron, for debt. 'Tis said his lordship had loaded pistols on the table at his side, but did not use them on the Poet's great grandsire. Of the Poet's boyhood days it is scarcely necessary to say much, only he was like some other boys, very full of mischief and mimicry, and could perform wonderful evolutions on his hands, by throwing himself over in windmill-like fashion, to the great amusement of his father's workmen. Besides this, he was considered rather witty for a youth, as the following incident will testify. At the Wesleyan Sunday School he attended, it was the custom of the elder boys, after morning school hours, to hurry into the chapel ; and as seats were not at all times easily to be found, they would hasten up the pulpit stairs, and, as many as could, sit there during the preaching service. But this thing had become a nuisance, not only in obstructing the preacher on his way to the pulpit, but also on account of the whispering going on during the discourse. This was made known to the teachers, who announced to the scholars that from henceforth the pulpit stairs were to be kept clear. On the following Sunday, however, before the teachers had left the school for the chapel, a boy, who was to be a poet, came running in, and told them there were twenty-four boys on the pulpit stairs already ; one of the teachers immediately hastened to expel the intruders, when, lo! to his astonishment, he found only two there. When these had been ordered down, he came back to the informant, and wished to know why he had dared to come and tell him there were twenty-four boys on the pulpit stairs. " Oh, sir," said he, " I will soon explain that. You know those two boys are the sons of Mr. Twelve, and that twice twelve are twenty-four !" This was too much for the teacher's risible faculties to hold, and he let the culprit go scot free that time. There are two other circumstances connected with his boyhood, which made at the time wonderful impressions on his mind, and are as fresh to-day as they were then—though more than fifty years have passed away ; one of them is as follows. Near the town in which he lived, it was currently reported that an otter had escaped from some place, and was making a temporary abode in an adjoining plantation, and a stream of water which flowed through it ; and at various times companies of young men had tried to secure it with dogs and other means they had at hand, but as yet it was all in vain. One Sunday morning, however, as a boy, who was to be a poet, was going to his Sunday school, he saw in the distance a number of young men coming towards him from the other end of the common, and the following thoughts, in the shape of question and answer, passed rapidly through his mind : " Who are these young men coming along ? Oh, I know. When I get near them I will ask them where they have been ; one of them, Richard Sanderson, will answer, ' We have been to hunt for the otter.' I shall then say, ' And have you caught it ? ' He will answer ' Yes.' I shall then ask, ' Where is it ? ' and he will answer " It is at Mr. Gilling's shop.' " When they all met, the same questions and answers as referred to were put and given by the same persons. What it was that brought all this about has been through the Poet's life an unravelled mystery. The other never-to-be-forgotten circumstance was as follows. One very stormy day, when he was about ten years old, he was standing in a large timber yard watching the sails of a neighbouring mill whirling rapidly round, when this premonition passed, as it were, in a moment through his mind : " The next time those sails go round, one of them will come off and dash through that maltkiln roof." The next time they went round one of them did come off, and went through that malthouse roof. Strange! yes, but true; and who can solve the problem?

The schooldays of the Poet were, on the whole, pleasant and agreeable to him, although not of long duration—for although his father had at that time a good business, yet it was an age when fathers believed in boys going to work early, and at the age of thirteen he had to earn his father, at wood-turning by piece work, ten shillings per week—what he earned over was his own for pocket money. When near the age of fifteen, however, his father thought he would apprentice him to the carpenter's business, for the following reasons. He was in the habit of purchasing large quantities of elm timber, for the seats of Windsor chairs : these were required to be of a certain size, and all timber, unless it reached that size, was practically useless, on account of its brittle nature, for any other parts of Windsor chairs ; and his father thought, by putting him to a carpenter, he would be able to find a use, in that trade, for what he himself could not turn to practical account. Consequently he was apprenticed to an industrious village carpenter, at Blidworth, on the hill near to Newstead Abbey, the seat of Lord Byron, and the spot where Dr. Livingstone wrote his last book. More than thirty years after this, he received congratulatory letters from the present owner of Newstead Abbey and his lady, for poems written on the death of Dr. Livingstone and his last words at Muilala, which appeared in several magazines, and are in this collection of poems. He immediately wrote back and thanked them for their courtesy and kindness in corresponding with him, and, however it might surprise them, it was nevertheless true, that the writer of the poems referred to was once a carpenter boy, and very near to Newstead Abbey. Since then he has had the pleasure and honour to visit Newstead Abbey, where a guide was furnished to conduct him to all its treasured spots ; and, on his leaving there, was presented with a spray from the tree on which Byron, at his last visit to Newstead, carved his immortal name ; and for which said bough that bore this inscription, the American speculating Barnum offered £500 to the then owner, Colonel Wildman ; who sent a polite message to the indomitable showman, on receiving it, that he would be obliged to Barnum if he would at once leave the Abbey grounds.

During the writer's visit to Newstead, he went to see Lord Byron's tomb, at Hucknal Torkard Church, where the kind old sexton paid him every attention, by procuring him a ladder to correctly copy the marble tablet there, by placing him on the exact spot under which Lord Byron lay ; " And," said the old man, " I assisted in placing Lady Lovelace, Byron's Ada, here."   Near the tablet were suspended wreaths, sent by eminent personages, to decorate the tomb of one of the greatest Poets of the age, and one who, had his mind been under Christian influence, might have been one of the most useful.   On this visit to Newstead and Byron's tomb, he had the great pleasure of meeting a number of friends at Blidworth, and spending a pleasant day, some of them being gentlemen he worked for when an apprentice boy ; and at night, at their request, he preached to them in the Wesleyan Chapel.

But to return to his apprentice days.   On his entering the village for the first time, he felt an unusual strangeness, for he felt like a stranger in a strange land ; and he will never forget the feeling that came over him the first night he crept into bed.   The fact was, it was not so comfortable, although clean, as the one he left behind him ; and he could not help thinking of " Home, sweet home," and his good old mother.   His apprentice days passed somewhat heavily, for he had

> Plenty of chopping and plenty of sawing,
> Plenty of planing and plenty of jawing,—

Because in those days country carpenters had often to

> Cut down very many trees,
> Which was not easy for the knees ;
> Then had to saw them up, alack !
> Which was not easy for the back.

And the Poet in his younger days has often walked eight miles per day, to and from his labour, carrying with him a large pitsaw, and by way of change, exchanging it with his fellow-apprentice for a carpenter's basket of tools.   Yet even then there was hope cheering him onward to Saturday night, when he would go and sit two quiet hours with one who was then all the world to him, and whose welcome company kept him from joining with the giddy and thoughtless of the village, and was one means of forming his character for life.

With her he spent thirteen years of happy married life, when, from a severe cold taken while on a visit with her husband to her widowed mother, she was somewhat prematurely taken to the home of no more dying, and the land of no more pain.

With four motherless children then was the Poet left, just when everything in life seemed to be opening out for him with a fair share of this world's prosperity. Yet during his apprenticeship he had one severe trial, namely, the loss of his dear father. A few short months before, he had seen him on his bed of affliction, and received from him his last fatherly advice, especially in reference to Intoxicating Drink,—which advice he has endeavoured to live out, by practical abstinence from all strong drink for now more than forty years, and for which he can never be too thankful, as through it he believes he has been enabled to accomplish an amount of mental labour he could never have performed otherwise.

One noontide, while coming from a near farmstead to his dinner, he found in his master's house one of his father's apprentices, who had walked seventeen miles that morning, bringing with him the heavy tidings that his father was no more. Then there was a departure for his home, where he had to meet for the first time a widowed mother. And then

> There was weeping within the old homestead,
> Where fond hearts had gathered of yore,
> By a widow bereft of her husband,
> And a lad who had father no more.

For in three short days a coffin was let down in his father's open grave. When the time of his apprenticeship had ended, he returned to his native town, and there by plodding industry he established a good business, for everything he seemed to put his hand to was successful; until unfortunately by listening to one—a lawyer, who came in the garb of a friend—he was induced to take steps which led to the enrichment of his apparent friend, and the ruin (for a time at least) of himself. The fruits of years of industry were swept away for the benefit of the spoiler, who to-day lies in an unenvied grave. For, after living some years in a luxuriant style on the hard earnings of others, his day of reckoning came. He was suddenly hurried from his stately mansion, and died like an exile at a wayside inn, on a neighbouring forest; and was taken from thence, 'tis said, to his burial, not in a richly plumed hearse, as 'twas once thought, but in a heavy farmer's cart. "God's mills grind slowly, yet their grinding's sure." Some time after the death of the Poet's first wife, he was sitting in the house of his eldest sister, when a friend of theirs entered, bringing with her a lady friend from Sheffield. When they had been seated for a while, he gave a casual glance at this strange lady, and in a moment there was a something seemed to say, "That will be your wife." Immediately he turned his head aside, and muttered to himself, "Impossible." Nevertheless, in a few months after this it was even so. While conversing with her some time after on this remarkable time, she said to her it seemed a mystery altogether. For on that day she entered Worksop, she had started from Sheffield with a few friends to visit a noted old ruin, not far from thence. When they reached the station, however, at which they intended to alight, she to the utter surprise of her friends said she would go forward to Worksop, and alone ; she had never been there before. They thought her conduct strange, and so did she, as she afterwards confessed. In the compartment of the carriage they occupied sat a lady, who told her that she also was going to Worksop, but going to see her friends ; and as she had seen her before near her own home, she would be glad if she would accompany her to her friend's house, where she would be welcome for the day. This offer was accepted, and with the results the reader has been made aware of. This second marriage of the Poet was happy, but of short duration, for she was in a decline, though she knew it not ; and in one year and ten months her husband had to follow her to the tomb. She sleeps in the beautiful cemetery at Sheffield, very near the honoured dust of James Montgomery, the Christian Poet ; and their little angel boy, whom they named after him, sleeps at Dronfield, a few miles away ; but his pure spirit has joined his mother's, and "that sweet singer's in the skies." The ways of Providence in this world are past finding out, for here was one who had become attached to his four motherless children, and who appeared to care for them as though they were her own ; and yet the homestead was again in mourning through the ravages of the king of terrors—death. It was during this sad bereavement that the poem, "Kilton Wood," was penned, although the writer had but written a few stray poems before, and but very few after, until he came to Clifton, and stood one day on grand St. Vincent's height. Then it was that a something stirred within him he had never felt before, and from that day he has been what the *Bristol Mercury and Daily Post* truly designated him, "The indefatigable Clifton Poet." He has been instant in season, and I dare say out of season, to some who have no regard for what strikes at evil and encourages what is right. His poem on "Kilton Wood" was published with a few others, at the request of many friends, in his native town ; and the spot is oft visited by those who appreciate the sentiment it contains. There is just one pleasing incident in connection with this poem, which the writer feels he ought not to omit to mention. Some six or seven years ago, while at his poet's stand on Clifton Down, a rather elderly lady, with a young lady and gentleman, came up St. Vincent's Rocks. One placard on the Poet's stall bore the following inscription :—" Kilton Wood, and other poems." This arrested the attention of the elder lady, who came up and said, "Will you please allow me to look at Kilton Wood book ?" Of course this request was readily complied with, for the Poet saw in her the demeanour of a true born lady. When she had received it she opened it, read a little and then smiled, and held it out for the young lady and gentleman to look at, when they read and smiled. She then looked at the Poet, and exclaimed, "And did you know Kilton Wood ?" He answered, "Yes, it is near my childhood's home.", She smiled benignantly, and said, "It was near there I spent my sweet childhood's days. You knew Lord Surrey, did you not ? " "Certainly I did," the Poet cried. "He was my father," she said ; and after making her purchases she bade him good-bye. It was Lady Foley ; and the title, "Kilton Wood," had touched a something within her that reminded her of bygone years : for Kilton Wood was part of her parental inheritance, and near her childhood's home.

Some time after his last bereavement, and before he left his native town to come to Bristol, he was, with his young family, induced to take a third wife. Their meeting was somewhat peculiar, and they married in haste, yet never repented at leisure—for the longer they lived, the better they loved, until death came twelve years afterwards and separated them for a little while. It was soon after this his great sore trouble came, for which she knew her husband was innocent. He had been too confiding; and a few words from the district manager of a bank, who knew him well, will explain it all—and they are given here for the good of posterity. " Mr. G.," said he, " you have been too honest. Lawyers are our best customers—I tell you this in confidence; but never trust them !" These words are placed here very reluctantly, but they are true; and if they are the means of leading young, industrious tradesmen, to think and act with proper discretion, they will not have been written in vain. When the spider's web had been discovered too late, his wife came, with the affection of a true-hearted woman, and clasped him in her arms, saying, " Never mind, love, I will be true to you ; I will never forsake you." Nor did she, she was true in storm as in sunshine ; and nearly the last words she said to her husband on her death-bed—and which were more to him than thousands of gold and silver—were, " I have always found you faithful." As a woman she had qualifications of a superior order, for she had a smattering of five languages, had devoted much attention to the study of botany, drawing, astronomy, and to the construction of the human frame. She was also methodical and economical in everything she did ; in fact, she was far above her husband both in culture and in every way—and he told her so many times before their marriage. But it mattered not: she loved poetry, and she loved a poet —and she had him,

> With his trials and his cares :
> Spite of a few hungry bears,
> Who'd have stopp'd them if they could—
> They did try, but 'twas no good.

After the Poet's great loss, through the villany of one man whom he trusted as a child would its father, he put his tool basket on his shoulder, and walked more than eight miles per day; and never lost one day for more than three years, at Walbeck Abbey woodyard, under His Grace the Duke of Portland. During this time he had again got together a nice little home, and made it more attractive than his neighbours': inasmuch as the minister of the church to which they belonged said one day when entering it, "Yes, Mrs. G.; your husband has been trying to make you comfortable here. But this is not your rest." Strange words, but true: for in a few short weeks the snug little home had to be left with its nice little garden, and pleasant look-out; and off for Bristol went the Poet. The reason of this sudden transition came about in the following manner. Early one morning, while in bed, he said somewhat suddenly to his wife, "I wonder, love, whether we shall ever live in Bristol?" What made him say it, he cannot tell, only he knows that it is true; and it so surprised his wife that she exclaimed, "Whatever, love, made you think of this?" He told her he did not know—nor did he; for, under the circumstances, he was very comfortable in his present place of employment—and, for aught he knew, there would be work for him there for an unlimited time. A few days after this, a letter was received by his dear wife from a friend in Liverpool, who owned an hotel at which commercial travellers called. He stated in that letter that a traveller, representing a Bristol firm, had been inquiring of him, to know if he could recommend a steady, trustworthy man, to take charge of a timber-yard belonging to a cabinet manufactory. His duties would be to take charge of the timber, and furnish certain quantities to the workmen, for the articles of furniture they had to make. He told him he did know of one whom he was sure would fill such a situation; and from future correspondence, and testimonials furnished, the situation was secured. The reason of the change was this—it was the wish of his wife, and the reason she gave appeared right. She said, "We are comfortable now, but the time will come when you will not be so strong as you are now—your constant walk of eight miles a day will tell on you by-and-by. Accept this situation in Bristol: you will have better wages, not so much hard work, and have more opportunities for bettering your position." He yielded to his wife's solicitation ; and one cold morning in the month of March, 1864, he left his native town for a city noted for its many churches, orphan houses, varied charities, and neglect of poets. It was night when he reached old Bristol, and all appeared to him gloomy enough —for the rain was pouring down in torrents. However, he managed to find the locality where his place of business was, and went into a coffee tavern nigh at hand, where he found comfortable lodgings and a home. Their minister had prayed, before he left his home, that he might find a comfortable place of abode, until his wife joined him ; and he did, with an elderly Christian widow, with one son at home, who, alternately with the Poet, conducted family worship there until his wife joined him. Early the next morning he hurried to his duties, and on entering the timber-yard for the first time, such a scene presented itself to his view as he hopes never to witness again : for the yard was in a complete upset, and the rain was pouring down ; whilst a sorry mixture of bricks and mahogany, mortar and American birch, mud and walnut, filth and rosewood, muck and maple, stones and pine-boards, met his vision ; and the eye of his mind went back to his clean, comfortable bench at Walbeck woodyard, and he almost wished himself there again. But he thought, " Well, I am here, and must try to make the best of it ; it will perhaps be better by-and-by—I will try to let them see I can make things look different soon." And he did, for his employer, who was an acute Scotchman, and did many people brown beside the Poet, congratulated him upon the change there was for the better in his timber-yard. But matters did not remain in this state long : as the Poet, before many weeks were over, discovered there was a screw loose, or a number of them, somewhere : for there came out in one of the daily papers, with whom the manufacturer largely advertised, a most glowing description of the said establishment and its workings, from tip to toe. One that made the Poet think, when he had read it, that it must have been a

Tremendous effort of the scribe's,
Unless he had some heavy bribes.

And he intimated as much in a letter to his wife, who had prudently arranged to stay behind to see how matters went on before the home was broken up, and the goods removed to Bristol. As he thought, so it came to pass. But a short time before it did, the manager came to him privately and said, "I hope, Mr. G., you will not think of bringing your goods to Bristol on the strength of our governor's promise, for I do assure you he is not to be trusted; and I do not wish you, a stranger, to be led away by him. He is continually advertising in the public papers for men, and when the poor fellows come, he has nothing for them; and in many instances we have had to make collections amongst ourselves to send them back to their homes." The Poet thanked him kindly for the information, and told him he should not be the worse for giving it, nor will he: for he has done serving employers who have no more regard for their workmen than the dirt, only as far as their selfish interests are served; and he is resting where the wicked cease to trouble, and the weary are at rest. Soon after the information was given the bubble burst, and the Poet was sent adrift; and what step to take he hardly knew, but at once wrote home to his sensible wife for instructions. She was very much surprised at the news, after the very flattering promises that had been made as to the permanence of the situation. Nevertheless, she wrote back at once, and her husband adhered to her advice. It was as follows: "To seek out for some present employment, and then be looking after a situation" she felt he ought to have: for she argued, "To come back to your old place, you would have the same amount of walking to do every day, and you are not growing younger;" and then she concluded her letter with these words: "I feel that the Lord has a work for you to do in Bristol." This last declaration of hers was decisive, and he went to Mr. F., a large building contractor near Brunswick Square, stated his case, and showed him testimonials of character he had brought from gentlemen of influence in his native town; and the one received from the firm he had come to Bristol for. When the gentleman had read these he looked at the Poet, for he was respectably dressed; and before he had time to speak, for he thought the gentleman was concluding he was too well-dressed to be fond of work, he said: " Oh, never mind, sir, my clothes; I am not afraid to labour. I have done a great deal of hard work in my time, and can do a great deal more yet." The gentleman immediately smiled, and said, "Well, you may come on to-morrow. We are building two villas near St. Matthew's Church. You can work there until something turns out better for you." The Poet wrote off at once and told his wife, and then she prepared to come to Bristol, bringing with her their youngest boy, and leaving his two daughters in situations near their mother's friends, and his eldest son in employment in that locality. These four children were by his first wife, two of whom are yet living—his eldest son and youngest daughter; while his eldest daughter Mattie, and his youngest son Fred, two years ago passed away to rest. Soon after his wife's arrival in Bristol she began to grow feeble, and medical aid being procured, it was found that she was suffering from cancer in the breast; and after lingering with its pain and discomfort for seven years, she calmly passed away. Nearly the last words her husband heard her repeat the night before, while conversing with her on death, were: " Jesus can make a dying bed feel soft as downy pillows are." On the next morning at seven o'clock, after he had left her much as usual at a quarter to six, he was fetched from his office at Keynsham, where he was managing a business. She had fallen asleep in Jesus. A short time before her death she had come into possession of a small cottage property at Sutton Bridge, in Lincolnshire, her native place. This she had made over by will to her husband with her own hand, and which since her death—for he never touched a shilling before, for he felt it was hers—he has been using in bringing out his little books, and but for this he would have been at the end of the chapter long ago; for the world has yet to learn that a Poet who writes for the good of humanity should be supported while he is doing his work. Providence, however, has enabled him to use this little money, so that what he has done, although not remunerative now, will be of service to his family when he is gone. It is for this, among other reasons, that he is keeping at his work, believing in an adage he has often given to many questions on this subject, that *doing right always pays*. His being left a widower the third time was not in itself so distressing as in the other instances, for as by some providential arrangement his daughter Mattie, who was over twenty years of age, had come home only a few months before her stepmother's death. She had not been strong for some time, and she wrote home and told them so. Her stepmother said at once she should come home, and her father wrote and told her this, hoping the change might do her good. Then she came, and it was while Mattie was at Keynsham growing stronger, that her stepmother passed away. During the time her mother had Mattie with her she was pleased, for she discovered a something in her that she loved, and nearly her last request to her husband was : " Father, buy Mattie a harmonium with my money when I am gone." She had discovered that there was in Mattie an ear and love for music, and her wish was complied with ; while oft at eventide and on the Sabbath has the Poet's mind been cheered by the music of his Mattie, who seemed to know when the tune of " Shall we gather at the river ? " and " There is a better land above," would be welcome to her sire. For some time she continued housekeeper for her father at Keynsham, where they were very happy together ; and thought that even there would be their dwelling-place for the residue of their days ; but there is nothing certain underneath the sun, for the business he was overlooking then was given up, and the Poet had to seek out for somewhere else to go. Before he left Bristol to overlook that business, his employer told him if he was not comfortable he was to come back—there was the same place for him again ; but he was comfortable at Keynsham, for during the five years he was there his employer and himself never had one unpleasant word ; and had it not have been for an unfortunate building speculation, he would undoubtedly have been there yet. But on being free to go, he went and laid his case before the gentleman whom he had left previously. He told him to come at once and resume his duties. Then there was another removal of his goods and another home to make. This was done very near to Clifton Down, where all went on pleasantly for a time, when all of a sudden this employer gave up his building business, and removed to Weston-super-Mare. The reason for this, it is told, was the following : He had formerly purchased a large quantity of land near to Stoke Bishop, and intended filling it with new villas ; and this being discovered by a neighbouring gentleman, who found out that some of them, which were to be in close proximity to his own mansion, would not only lessen its value, but be a continual annoyance to himself, he after a deal of change ringing on both sides, bought up all the land and unfinished villas, and thus put a stop there to the building operations of the Poet's employer. He himself told the Poet that the other party had had many opportunities of purchasing the land before, and cheap. They had let the opportunity slip, and now had to purchase it very dearly. This evidently was true, for it enabled the builder to appear like the gentleman, although for aught he seemed to care his workmen might become beggars ; for there was no temporary provision made for them until they could secure employment elsewhere, as all the work was stopped at a few hours' notice, and the Poet sent adrift again. For weeks after this he was trying to procure an over-looker's situation, but nothing seemed to turn up, although he was in the meantime doing his best to turn something up himself ; for he paced Bristol city day after day till he was tired, footsore, and faint. He advertised in the public papers for a place of trust and responsibility, but nothing came ; and yet while all this was going on, kind friends were saying : " I am sure there are scores of gentlemen who would put you in a good situation, if they knew." Well, many of them did know, and a few of them exercised their influence ; but it did not come to pass, until one day he determined in the following week to go and seek work as a journeyman carpenter, and try to do what good he could in a quiet way on a Sunday. On the Sunday morning following this resolve he had to go out into the country to preach twice ; and it being a very rainy morning, he put on a pair of boots with thicker soles than those he usually wore, and what with hurrying over Kingsdown, and the slippery state of the roads, on his way to meet the conveyance at the bottom of the hill, he had a fearful fall ; and although it did not entirely disable him, it made his left arm for a time powerless, though it was not dislocated. Nevertheless, it disqualified him for working at the bench for a time, had a situation been found for him. He went forward that morning, however, to his preaching duties ; took the service in the morning with his clothing all bespattered with mud, and his painful arm. Before the evening service, his friends with drying and brushing had made him more becoming to appear in public—although for the next few weeks he was for all laborious purposes comparatively useless. It was at this time that the Teignmouth Catastrophe occurred, on June 18th, 1874. An excursion from Bristol of the *employés* of Robinson and Co. went down to Teignmouth, when a party of young people went out for a short sail with a boatman who had unfortunately a boat that was unseaworthy : for when a short distance from the shore she began to fill with water, and in a short time all the occupants of the boat were in the sea—in sight of hundreds who could render them no assistance. The young men in the boat saved themselves by swimming to shore, with the exception of one Walter Lovell, aged 17. He also could have done this, but he heard the voice of one he was engaged to, Agnes Saunders, aged 17, calling from the water, " Walter ! Walter !" and he went back to try to save her ; but 'twas all in vain, and they died together, firmly clasped in each others' arms, and near them three more young lady friends. This sad occurrence filled the City of Bristol, from whence they started, with the most pungent grief ; and it was resolved to give them a public funeral. They were brought back to Bristol, and at their interment a most affecting and numerous procession wended its way to Arno's Vale. The Poet was among the spectators, and he felt acutely on the subject ; and that night and the next morning early, there were thoughts in reference to them rising from his soul. Then he hurried from his bed, nor did he rest until he had placed the Teignmouth Catastrophe Poem on his breakfast table. After breakfast, he read it to his daughter Mattie, who gave him her opinion of it in the following words : " Oh, that is good, father. Have a thousand copies printed ; and if they will but do good and pay the printer, we will be satisfied." It was just with that feeling it went to press, and it astonished both the Poet and the public, for in four weeks from its appearing in print, twenty thousand copies had been issued from the press, and most of them sold. This thrilling circumstance seemed to convey to the mind of the Poet this truth, " Now you are to have different employment from toiling with the plane and saw. Poetry is your work. Here is a proof. What you have written is evidence that your lines are appreciated by the public. You have heard that readers of this poem, at the windows of booksellers in the city, have in the public streets been moved to tears. This is your path. You will succeed, only persevere." And from that day to this he has been endeavouring to do this, very often amid many discouragements ; and had it not been for some encouraging words from men of mark, not only for worldly position, but mental culture, *and a sense of duty*, he would have given it up long ago. Soon after his " Teignmouth Catastrophe " poem came out, he published a number of others, which although not so remunerative as this, kept him clear of the printer's books ; and as they invariably inculcated good lessons, they were not written in vain. One day, while on St. Vincent's in summer-tide, he felt a something unusual stirring within him, and he sat down before the grand panorama, and penned his poem, " Cliftonia the Beautiful." The title of the poem was attractive, and being entirely new, it procured for it a ready sale. It struck the Poet just after he had written this poem, if he could but procure an engraving of the Suspension Bridge to place on the sheet with it, it would make it somewhat attractive, and help to sell the same ; yet how to obtain one was to him a mystery, for he had no experience in these matters. One day, however, before the poem was printed, he had the manuscript in his pocket; and shortly took a stroll near the Observatory, gazing on the matchless beauties of the scene. While there he thought he would take a seat for a short time, and just look over his manuscript again. While he was thus employed, a strange gentleman came and took a seat beside him. There they both sat silently for a time, until the stranger made some remarks on the magnificent scene that lay before them. Then the Poet told him he had been trying to depict the same in the poem that he held in his hand ; and he invited the gentleman to read it, who told him that

c

he always felt interested in descriptive poems. The Poet told him
that he had thought of having it printed, and had also thought, if he
could have an engraving of the Suspension Bridge to have gone with
it, that it would have been an advantage. He immediately replied,
" I am sure it would ; and I am an engraver from London, and shall
be pleased to do a nice one for you." Then there was an inquiry
about the price, and an appointment made to meet the Poet at his
home next day. At the hour appointed the stranger made his
appearance, and had not been long seated, when he looked across
the room to a framed steel engraving, and said, " I see you have
my father's likeness there." " Your father's!" exclaimed the
Poet. " Yes, the Rev. E. P." " Then," said he, " if that is your
father, he is my friend." The order for the bridge was given and
executed, and it is the one that appears on the eighteen forty-two
paged books already published by the Poet. Shortly after this
poem appeared a thought struck him, that if he could but be
allowed to exhibit his poems on Clifton Down, he would secure more
readers by getting them into the hands of strangers from distant
parts. He made application for permission to do so, sending
specimens of his poems, and a letter showing that what he was
writing was all pure literature ; and had in them what would be useful
to mankind. This letter secured for him the privilege to exhibit
them on Clifton Down on a Poet's stall. This was his first effort at
being his own publisher, and his first purchaser was C. Cordeux,
Esq., Jeweller, of Clifton. The reason he adopted this mode (for this
kind of work was all new to him) of being his own publisher, was
from information he met with in *Punch* years before he began his
strange avocation. The paragraph read as follows : " Did you ever
know an author who could have oyster sauce to his beefsteak ? Did
you ever know a publisher who couldn't?" " Ah !" thought the Poet,
" there is something in that paragraph worth looking at. If I am to be
an author I will be my own publisher ; it may be slower work at first,
but if there is any harvest worth gathering at the last, my family

Shall have the good of all my life sowing,
If their father should be pinch'd while the seed is growing."

There was one pleasing incident connected with the first appearance of the Poet's Stall on Clifton Down. A person of very gentlemanly demeanour from the Clifton Down Hotel passed by, and gave furtive glances at it; but did not venture to stay until he had gone by several times. Then he took up some of the leaflets, for as yet the Poet had not published one book. This gentleman read some of the pieces, one of which appeared very much to interest him. It was a production by the Poet's daughter Mattie, and her first, entitled "Love's reply to affection's question." He purchased all the copies of this on the stall, and a few others, and went away; but just as the Poet was closing his stall for the night, this same gentleman came to him with a beautiful book, and wished him to present it to his daughter, remarking, that a father who owned a child who could write such beautiful lines ought to be proud of her. The Poet told him he was thankful for her, and also very much obliged to him for the kind present he had brought her. The next morning, before the Poet had well arranged his stand, the same gentleman came up, making inquiries whether he had presented her with the book. The Poet told him he had, and that his daughter was very much obliged to him for it; and she also stated that if he would not deem it intrusive, she would be pleased to know who she had the honour of thanking for it. Immediately, the gentleman raised his hat and said, "Sir Godfrey L——." From that very hour there sprung up a Christian friendship between the baronet and Poet, and while he remained in Clifton—it was his favourite resort; for having, as he stated, travelled much, he admired Clifton for its scenery more than any place in the world—they had many a pleasant chat on travels, church matters, and other subjects; and when he left Clifton for his London home he came to bid farewell to the Poet, and his parting words were: "I have one thing more to say to you, Mr. G., persevere. What you write is good, and written for doing good. Persevere, your path will open some day." Then placing a gold coin in his hand he said, "That is to help you a little in your printing. Good-bye." The Poet took encouragement from this, not merely because the speaker was a baronet, but an author as well. It was at this time that the Poet had to wheel his poem stall one mile in the morning, and the same distance home at night, for it would not have been safe to have left it on Clifton Down for many reasons; but the time soon came when there was a way made for him to do it, and leave it well secured. One morning when he was wheeling it on his way from home, he was seen by Sir Godfrey, who came to him and said, "What a pity it is you should have so much labour to get your productions for sale." On another occasion while taking home his stall, he was accosted on the way by two would-be witty gentlemen, who wanted to know if what he was wheeling was a trough to feed sheep from. "Not exactly," said the Poet, "although I daresay there is some good food in it for both sheep and lambs." Some time after another gentleman met him with it on the road, and said, "Why, whatever is that,—is it for a coffin?" "No, sir," said the Poet, "but there is something in it which, if rightly used, will be of service to people in helping them to prepare for their coffins." The gentleman turned up his eyes at this, and off he went. One day some time after this, another gentleman, evidently of position, if diamond rings are an evidence when on the fingers, called at his publication stall, and took up several of his little books and looked them over; and then very sneeringly said : "You appear to be, by your books, rather religiously inclined." The Poet looked straight at him and said : "Yes, sir, rather; and if there is nothing after this life is ended, there is something in Christianity to cheer me on my journey; and at its ending I shall be no worse off than the unbeliever. But if there should be something more, and the Bible is true, where will the unbeliever be?" He said no more, but he did purchase a book, and went his way. On the Poet's first coming to Bristol, he had a somewhat encouraging incident in connection with his history. It was the time when Garibaldi the brave was about to visit England. Early one morning while in bed, he was thinking on the life work of the patriot, and in a few minutes he struck off some lines as a welcome to him, and dropped them into the receiving box for correspondence at the office of the *Bristol Mercury and Daily Post.* The next day they appeared in print, and a few days after the Poet was waited upon at the Cabinet Works, St. Philip's, by a gentleman from Park Street, music-seller to the Queen, asking if he would allow the words to be published with music, to which they had been set by Leigh Wilson, Esq. ; and they would like to have them published. He of course gave his consent, for there came as it were in a moment golden visions floating through his brain ; but poetlike these hopes were doomed to disappointment, as, although they were forwarded to their London publisher they were not published, for the following reasons, as stated by Mr. C. himself: " When the lines and music arrived in London, our publisher had another on the same subject in the press ; and it was thought to publish both would injure the sale of one—although we consider that yours are the best stanzas." The Poet felt himself flattered at the frank confession, and more particularly so as the one in the press was the composition of that true Poetess, Eliza Cook. It was a short time after this that he wrote his " Blind Boy " poem. It was written a few weeks after he came to Bristol, on Sunday during the intervals of public worship, in a chamber at his lodgings, with the old Christian widow lady in St. Philip's, opposite the Avonside Engine Works ; and its subject is his own life experience. He is somewhat particular in mentioning these circumstances in reference to this poem, because it has been extensively and usefully circulated ; and also graciously accepted by Her Majesty the Queen. But to return to his little book, or rather poem stall, on the Down, for he had not yet written one book ; and his first was brought out under somewhat painful circumstances, and entitled, " Musings Poetical from the Diary of Miss Chameleon Circumstances." Owing to a severe attack of lumbago, brought on by sheltering from the rain and snow in an old cold stone cave or grotto, near the Poet's tree, some of the stanzas of this book were composed at home while he lay in the easiest position he could find— namely, on the boarded floor of his room. This book was graciously accepted by Her Royal Highness the Princess of Wales, and the first edition of one thousand being sold, a second edition of two thousand more came from the press, with an engraving of Her Royal Highness on the cover. His next venture was the " Blind Boy," and other poems. A second edition of this book of two thousand also has come out; his third book was "The Good Wife at home : scenes from the life of John and Martha Careful." This book has been much praised, its object being to show that a British workman's wife is in her right place at home, and that her husband and family are more benefited by her being there than going out to work. This book has been pronounced excellent by the Editor of the *British Workman*, who had the manuscript for review. The Poet was requested to have it printed ten years before it was published, having given it from memory at several social gatherings, for it was one of his earliest productions. His "Kilton Wood" book came next, and then "Uncle Peter," dedicated to juvenile and non-juvenile smokers : the eleven chapters are experiences in the Poet's history. The first scene in it occurred before a large mansion with lodge that once stood opposite the entrance to Barton Regis, Eastville; and with the exception of a little innocent filling up, the incidents are all true. The Poet received the personal thanks of S. Morley, Esq., for its production, copies of which he purchased to go to London, and one of the Laureate's brothers came, and introduced himself by fetching one; and after perusing it said : "This is a good book, although I am a notorious smoker." From that time they became friends, and on his leaving Clifton, where he was then residing, he brought the Poet a parting present of "Thomson's Seasons." Many a pleasant and profitable chat had they together before this on Clifton Down, for he was a believer in the teaching and doctrines recorded in the good Old Book; and on one occasion he brought one of his brothers to introduce to him, and since then another has been, and brought with him two interesting young ladies, his own daughters, to see the once carpenter boy; and Lord Tennyson himself has sent him an autograph letter, with thanks, for his book "Evangeline;" and the Right Hon. the Earl of Shaftesbury as well. There is one encouraging incident in the publication of this little book, it may be right to mention here. A Clifton gentleman who had passed by the stall for many years without having turned aside except to just give a nod of the head to the Poet, one night as he was closing did so, and said, "Mr. G., will you let me have one of your little books to look at." He was told, certainly. Then he said, "Let me have your best, if you know it." The Poet said to him, "Please to read 'Evangeline.'" He took it, and the next morning early he was up at the Poet's stand; and the first words he said were: "You have surprised me." "Surprised you?" said the Poet. "Why?" "Oh!" said he, "I never thought you had written anything equal to this." "Well, sir," the writer exclaimed, "you well know that you never came near me to see." The gentleman then said, "Why, this poem should be in every drawing-room in the land. It is better worth one and sixpence than to be in a threepenny book. If you will bring it out in a nice little book by itself for drawing-rooms, and it does not pay you, I will make good your loss." At the request of this gentleman, it has been brought out in a nice form, and published at sixpence. He has received many flattering letters on this book; and one lady who visits Clifton every year, and comes for the Poet's last new books, said she felt that she must come back and tell him how pleased she had been to read "Evangeline." Another lady wished to know from him, if he did not feel proud with such a gift. He told her, "No!" What had he to feel proud of? It was only a gift bestowed upon him by the Almighty, and one which he felt he would have to be accountable for the right using of. It might be made very useful, or very dangerous. It was a power for good or evil, and he had determined that all his writings should be like Miss Hannah More's, only for battling with wrong and establishing right. Many people thought her mad for a time; but there was method in her madness, and Providence in her last days had rewarded her for her adherence to principle. His book, "Excelsior: a day dream on St. Vincent's Rocks," the first poem of which portrays his own life, has received a fair share of attention, for it has in it an impromptu written for that popular American Poet, Will Carleton, who spent two hours with the Clifton Poet, underneath his tree, in summertide—and whom his American brother told it was like coming into a new world to find him there; and they parted reluctantly, perchance never to meet again on earth. That book also contains the last complete poem of his dear daughter Mattie, on the death of our Princess Alice. One day a stranger passed the Poet's stall, and took this little book with him to London. He was the father of a musical composer there. When his son had seen in it two new songs, entitled " My Mother," and " Minnie Ray," he wrote at once to Clifton, for the Poet to write him some pieces to set to music. This he did on several occasions, and always received from him not only congratulation, but remuneration also. The most successful book as yet, in point of circulation, of the Poet's, is one entitled " Cook's Folly : a Legendary Ballad of St. Vincent's Rocks," and written there one summertide, on a piece of board behind the Poet's stall. The first edition was sold in sixty-two booksellers' shops in Bristol and Clifton alone. It has passed through three editions, and the fourth will soon be out. This book has had a glowing review from the *Western Temperance Herald*, and was patronised by the late owner, H. Goodeve, Esq., J.P., who sent a good order, and an autograph letter with it. The Poet has deemed it right to publish this story complete in this volume, with engraving of Cook's Folly, as it is the world-renowned legend of " Cliftonia the Beautiful." His book, " Isabel and I : an Old Man's Christmas Story," and other poems, has not been so much inquired for as some other of his books that are not equal to it for touching incident. The Poet gave it as a reading one Christmastide, to a crowded congregation in a large chapel, and had the pleasure of hearing it said by some ladies, that they could have sat another hour if the story had but continued ; and one Sunday, while seated at a farmhouse in the country, where he had gone to preach, the good lady of the house, in the afternoon, was reading the story to some friends, when she became so affected that she sobbed aloud, and had to lay the book down for another friend to finish it for her. Some time before this the Poet received a beautifully bound volume of poems from a popular poet at Lymington, — Doman, Esq., and also a very interesting letter, in which the author gave the following pleasing testimonial :—" We keep your little books on our table, Mr. G., and read them with much interest ; especially ' Isabel and I.' " The Poet's book, " Miss Nancy Dare," was brought out for the special purpose of showing the wilful ways of some young ladies, who dare to do what they please, as this young lady did. Nevertheless, it is shown in this humorous production that in time she became wiser, and made a very excellent wife, when *she dared to do right.* His book, " Marion's Joy," has been much appreciated, and no doubt will continue to be, when the writer has passed away. A clergyman of the Church of England, and of long experience, did the Poet the honour of saying that the story would immortalise Leigh Woods for ever. It is a true love story, and the lessons taught in it are more valuable than nine-tenths of the flaming novels of the age. It was at this time, while the Poet was busy with his labour, feeling that the more he wrote the more he must, he had to undergo one of the most painful trials of his life, namely, the loss of his dear daughter Mattie. For ten years she had been his little housekeeper, and, in all that she could, she had done her best to fill the place of her foster-mother. Consumption—that deadly foe of her own mother—touched her. Alas! and just at the time when she appeared to be beginning to live, she had to die. She had just begun to write some interesting poems, and being a district visitor for some time at Redland, had opportunities for making observations, which she was turning to good account. She had begun to bring out the Clifton penny series, " Pure ballads for the nation." Her first, " Tommy Macarthy ; or, lost and found," is a true incident, and Mattie was the person who led the poor young Irish mother from Redland Park that night, to find her little one cared for by the kind policeman at Clifton Down reserve. Her next little book, " Nellie Rae," is very much admired. Her father one day received a glowing letter from a strange gentleman in one of the Oxford Colleges, stating that " Nellie Rae " had been sent him by a friend ; how much he liked it, for it was calculated to do much good, and he hoped it would have an extensive circulation. A gentleman also in Clifton, from St. John's College, Cambridge, told Mattie's father that she reminded him more of Mrs. Browning than any writer he had ever read ; and yet she was brought up in a country village, after the loss of her mother, with an aunt, with scarcely any advantages for culture or refinement, which seemed to be so very essential for her. When she began to write a few poems, her father, to encourage her, had inserted in his threepenny books a few of her own productions. Her first piece, " Love's reply to affection's question," "We shall meet her once again," " Our Princess Alice," " Emily portrayed," " The angels mind him now," these she would oft read over to her father, as he oft did to her his own ; and this was done for the mutual advantage of them both. She had another little book in hand at the time of her death, entitled " Patty Cree's angel whisper." This was her own life history; and, strange to say, before she had concluded it, the angels whispered her away. At her request her father finished it for her, she giving him what she wished to be inserted in reference to her, and it is now added to her penny series. Long before she appeared to be sinking, this thought would oft come across her father's mind, " Who would perform those duties for her at such a time, that he felt only a loving mother could bestow upon her child ? " Could he have but known what afterwards came to pass, such thoughts need never to have troubled his mind: for in her affliction she had every attention from many kind friends, who valued her for her quiet and unobtrusive spirit, and who had been touched by the simple pathos of her lays. On the 16th day of June, 1880, she sweetly fell asleep in Jesus, without a struggle or a sigh ; and dying, as she wished, in her father's arms. She rests, at least what is mortal of her, at Keynsham, Somerset, in the same burial ground as the Poet's third wife. After this great loss he had to keep himself more than ever diligently employed at his writing, lest his mind should become desponding under the trial; and for a time he wrote almost incessantly to give him heart relief for a father's pungent grief. His little book, " What News is the Postman bringing to-day ? Ten scenes from real life," came out soon after, which is being read with interest, and appreciated by soldiers and sailors ; some of the incidents being true—for the Poet with his varied life experiences seems to be never short of subjects to write upon. The great difficulty with him at times was, which to select, and so to use them as to make them useful, and also to pay him for their publication. And he will never forget the heartfelt gladness of a poor old widow who had a boy at sea, after she had read his No. 2 sketch in the above named little book. And some time ago he had a letter from a ship's captain for some of his books, and who told him how much they were prized by the men aboard ship. His book, " The Poet's Tree ; or, secrets of a year," will always be interesting to those who read it. This book was written to give an account of many influential personages who had been under the tree where the Poet had his stall, and their varied conversations with him. The idea was taken from the Laureate's " Talking Oak," he thinking that by this means he might show the object of his mission ; and also the varied treatment he had received there, while trying to carry it out. " Howe'er it be, it seems to me " that he has in some measure immortalised the tree, for the little book is being much read, and leaves from it are being taken to the four quarters of the globe. In this collection of poems, the faded leaf and its lessons is a true story, and there are many more of a similar character that may be published some day in connection with the Poet's tree ; for the Poet, during the eleven years he has been under the shadow of it, has come in contact with more varieties of character than in all the former periods of his life ; and if there should be found a doubter of this statement, the Poet would advise them, if they want convincing, to open a publication stall for the same number of years with their own productions only ; and he feels assured that before half the time is expired, these would readily admit that what Thomas Carlyle said of the generality of human kind, was not an immeasurable distance from the truth ; for there the Poet has had such a variety of minds to contend with, and a great deal that was not mind at all, but a something that is always calculated, in the age where useful intelligence may be obtained, to irritate and annoy any person with ordinary common-sense.

> For 'tis indeed, though some are sage,
> A very nickel silver age ;
> And poets would have glad surprise,
> If some folk would become more wise.

Some time after this, the Poet wrote and brought out his book on " God's Orphan Homes," Ashley Down, Bristol. He had oft longed to write a book on this Christlike institution, but seemed as if he could never get on with it until he went through the whole five houses and saw the wonderful provision made for the 2,050 orphans there; and after he had seen them at their varied employments and enjoyments, he felt he could have written anything that was good in reference to them. He had three reasons for writing this book. One was, he thought, that it might receive a fair share of attention, and repay him for its publication. Another was, he had been asked, by ladies and gentlemen visiting Clifton, for full information respecting them, and he could not give it; and therefore thought, if he could personally visit them, go into every room, and put in verse every particular, he could then tell them he had been and seen; and, if they thought well to have his little book for threepence, it was all there. The third reason was, he thought, that he could so write it, that the Almighty might in His own way influence the minds of the wealthy and others to visit the Homes, and thus coming in contact with the happy orphans, would help those who were in a measure helpless, from a sense of duty to Him who was the Bestower of their wealth. The Poet deems it right to state here, that in composing and bringing out this book, he had no solicitations from any of the conductors, or Mr. Müller himseff. He wrote it from a sense of duty, and just because he felt he must; it has been the means of many going there, and will be again. A very wealthy lady in Clifton, who had purchased one of the Orphan Home Books, came to the Poet and said, " I have read your charming little book; I feel I must now go through the Homes—tell me the best way to go there." And so it is Providence uses man as an instrumant for the accomplishment of its purposes. But the age has yet to learn that we are to live by each other for the true purposes of life, and not on each other for our own selfish aggrandisement. There have been at times under the Poet's tree some very singular incidents; and it may be right here to refer to a few of them. One very hot summer's day, three gentlemen came to overlook the Poet's stand. They had on new fashionable straw hats with white streamers attached. They could not see anyone in charge of the stall, for the Poet was con-

cealed behind it, writing in the shade. After passing varied remarks
on the unusual things before them, one of the gentlemen evidently
had his attention drawn to some photos of the Poet in the glass case
before him : for he observed rather jocularly to his companions, if the
photographer, when he took that face, thought he was photographing
a fool, he made a grand mistake. The Poet smiled at this remark
in his hiding-place, and remained there until they went rejoicing on
their way. The Clifton Poet's political views and proclivities are
well known in the locality where he resides. Although he has always
avoided parading them before the public at his Publication Stall,
unless he has been compelled to do so by those entertaining opposite
opinions, he has had for some time two distinguished names there of
gentlemen who have accepted his productions, and on this account
he has been often twitted by some peculiar gentlemen. The names
referred to are those of the Hon. W. E. Gladstone and the Hon.
J. Bright. A singular gentleman once, in passing and observing
them, said, " Mr. G., those are the wrong names for Clifton." " Never
mind, sir," said the Poet ; " they seem to be right for the country."
At another time a stranger to the Poet passed, although from his
frequent appearance in that locality he might be a resident or constant
visitor. He was very tall and somewhat consequential in appearance,
and was invariably sucking a cigar. This morning he said somewhat
haughtily to the Poet, " I understand that you are a supporter of Mr.
Gladstone." The Poet answered, " I am a supporter, sir, of everyone
who is trying to do right ; and it is for this reason alone that I am
a supporter of Mr. Gladstone." He said no more, but went from the
Poet's stall down old St. Vincént's Hill, looking as pleasant as an old
crab-tree, or, to use one of the Poet's father's expressions, as if " he owed
him a quarter's rent." It was the selfsame gentleman to whom the
impromptu " Served him right," in this collection, was written ; for the
incident was true. Another time, at the Industrial Exhibition held
at Hotwells, Clifton, the Poet had a stall to exhibit his productions ;
and in order to make it as attractive as possible without any
design of exhibiting his political views, he had among a few noted
philanthropists and popular ministers of Bristol for whom he had written

"In Memoriams," and of one notable woman, Miss Mary Carpenter. In the centre of these was an incentive acrostic in gilt frame, to the Right Hon. W. E. Gladstone on his 71st Birthday. It was written as a grateful recognition of his restoration to health, with the hon. gentleman's photo in the centre, and two mottos, one on the left the other on the right hand, "I will guide thee with Mine eye; and, "As thy day, so shall thy strength be." It was the counterpart of one sent as a present to Hawarden Castle, and while in the exhibition, from right thinking people, had its meed of praise. But one day, while this was on the Poet's stall, a very influential lady in the locality came and took a survey of the books, &c., there; and he, without thinking he was doing anything wrong, said: "This is Mr. Gladstone's Birthday Poem." "Yes!" she tartly answered, "and it ought to be burnt, and him too." Such a reply naturally surprised the Poet, and looking her full in the face, he said: "You will excuse me, madam; but you will have to get all such feelings out of your heart, or you will never enter into the kingdom of heaven." She immediately bowed her head and said: "I beg your pardon, sir, I feel that I have done wrong." "Done wrong!" said he. "Yes; you, Mr. G., may have made mistakes, as we all have—for we are but human." "But a close observer of his history cannot fail to discover that his whole life service has been devoted to the true interests of his country and the universal welfare of mankind." Many similar instances of annoyance has the Poet had to contend with by having placed on the inside leaves of his book copies of some lines he had placed on his poem stand to induce strangers to stay and give them their attention. Ladies and gentlemen desired to have copies of them, and to meet their wishes, these were inserted for a time inside the covers of his little books. One of the lines read thus,

"The honoured names of Gladstone, Bright;"

and, strange to say, that single line has caused the Poet more annoyance from some people than all the poems he has written—not from right-minded people, he admits: nevertheless, it has been even so. One day a lady came to the Poet's stall, bringing with her a young lady, evidently her daughter; having purchased some of his books, they went and sat down upon the grass underneath the Poet's tree, and the elder lady began to read aloud to the other. After having read several of the poems, the Poet approached her, and said, "You will excuse me, madam, but you know how to read poetry—it is a pleasure to hear you : for there are some persons who make such a muddle of it, that it gives me the horrors to hear them." The lady smiled, and said she was fond of good poetry. She was then going back to Ireland with her daughter, and they had come up St. Vincent's heights for a short time, to have a look round whilst waiting for the starting of the steamboat. She then exclaimed, "I suppose you think highly of Mr. Gladstone?" The Poet replied that he did, but that had nothing to do with his books : Mr. G.'s name was there with others simply because they had accepted his productions. She then said, "I feel that I could shoot him for what he has done in reference to disestablishing the Irish Church." The Poet immediately looked straight at her, and said, "Oh, no! you could not. I see, in your face, that you would not shoot anyone, especially Mr. Gladstone." She immediately broke out into a fit of laughter, and said, "Oh, yes ; I could, though !" And then they had lengthy conversation on the Irish Church and the Irish people ; and before they parted, she frankly confessed that she believed eventually it would be a real benefit : for the Protestant clergy, now more than ever, felt that they had important work to do, and therefore must do it. Since that time, the lady has on several occasions come from Dublin to Bristol ; but never fails to come and see the Poet, and take back with her a few of his little books. On another occasion he had a contention that afforded him some amusement, with two apparently maiden ladies, who had been at his stall a few days before, and purchased some of his little books. On the following day they came to see the Poet, and wished to know if he would exchange one of them for one of another kind : they liked the book, only there was Mr. Gladstone's name in it, and that they did not like. The Poet cheerfully exchanged the book, and then wished them to give him their reasons. This they commenced doing with great volubility : for the dear old souls opened out their minds freely and fully ; but Mr. G.'s chief offence, in their opinion, was that he was in league with the Pope, and someone else whom they did not scruple to name. They were horror-struck to contemplate what the country would come to by-and-by, if he continued at the head of affairs. Then the Poet tried to get a word in edgeways, which was a most difficult thing to do. He did his best to show them that even they might be mistaken, and that Mr. G. was not half so ugly as they had tried to paint him. But no, no! the dear old ladies could not see it ; they had got their peculiar glasses on, and consequently the Poet had to let them have it all their own way. When they had walked on, he sat down and wrote the poem, " What a wonderful age we live in."

To mention all the amusing and remarkable incidents in connection with the life of the Poet while on Clifton Down, would swell this autobiography to a larger size than he deems would be prudent to accompany a collection of poems ; and therefore he wishes to select only those that may be serviceable to posterity—showing them that the path of a Poet is not a smooth path ; and to inculcate one important lesson that the present age seems slow to learn, namely, that it is while a Poet is doing his work in life, he needs helping and caring for; and especially when he his battling with the evils of the age, and trying to uplift mankind into a purer, nobler, and a better life. And yet there are such to-day who are trying to do this, who do not meet with as much pecuniary assistance as many a crossing sweeper; and why? The Clifton Poet thinks it is because folk don't agree to live a life of purity. If they did, why don't they help to circulate that which under the Divine blessing and guidance would help to promote it? One day, while he was on Clifton Down, a group of ladies and gentlemen came past the Poet's tree ; and seeing the inscription near it, one of them inquired if that was Chatterton's tree. " No, sir," said the Poet; "the books on this stall are my own productions only, and I have written a book on this tree. That is the reason it is named the Poet's tree." When they heard this, they looked at the Poet in astonishment, as though they had expected seeing an angel with wings, instead of an ordinary mortal ; and then one of them exclaimed : " Oh ! we have not time to stay and look at them now." " No, sir," said the Poet; " and if Chatterton himself had been here, it would have been just the same, and that is what the Poets have to contend with here—

> Doing their work, sitting alone,
> Giving full many a sigh and a groan ;
> Thoughtless ones passing them giving a grin,
> Never once caring what plight they are in."

The very exposed position of the Clifton Poet's stall to the elements has been no small source of trial in addition to the before mentioned circumstances, for he has been without any kind of shelter, with the exception of an old stone grotto near his stall, and in which he has written scores of poems while the rain and snow have been rapidly falling, and beating on his feet. For eleven years he has been thus toiling, and, he has thought, sufficiently long to have exhausted the patience of any man, unless he had faith in his mission. A Catholic gentleman, who had at different times purchased the Poet's books, not only for himself, but for friends who had come to visit Clifton, one day while passing the Poet's stall remarked : " Mr. G., the Clifton ladies ought to put you here a pretty little Poet's shelter ; and have felt it an honour to have such a man in their midst. That is what I think." " Well, sir," the Poet answered ; " many of them yet don't seem to understand a Poet's work. Had I have driven a cab or had a wheel-chair, I have no doubt it would have been done long ago ; but they have yet to learn that a man who is spending the latter part of his life in writing books to lead folk to nobler, purer, and better life, is of as much use to society as the man who drives a horse." He answered, " You are right," and then he went his way ; while the Poet hummed over a line of one of his favourite poems :

> It seemeth to me a shame it should be,
> In a beautiful world like this.

The storms that so frequently beat upon St. Vincent's Rocks have at times proved very disastrous to the Poet, in driving over his stall, and many times sending his leaflets to the four winds of heaven. One day especially was very trying. The day previous he had the misfortune to have a breakdown with the wheel upon which he used to convey his stall at night for protection behind the rocks. Then he had to go a long journey into the city—east, west, north, and south, to find another, which he thought a suitable one. At length he appeared to have succeeded, and brought it early in the morning, and fixed it to the stall, ready as he thought for service next time. When it was tried, it brought him safely up the hill. It was, however, no sooner at the top, than the wind began to blow in hurricanes, so much so that he dare not venture to open it out, nor dare he venture to take it back, until some hours after, when the wind had a little abated. While it did so he fled to his old stone cave for protection, for the storm seemed fierce enough to tear up the very trees by the roots. When three o'clock came the Poet made an effort to try to bring his stall to a place of shelter. He was on his way down the hill, wheeling it as he thought safely, although he himself could scarcely stand upright in the tempest, when all of a sudden the new wheel broke down, and of course down went the stall on its side ; and off went the Poet's hat, while he was clinging to his crippled companion with all the energy of despair. For some time he was in this immovable position, until some unknown friends in the distance, seeing how matters stood, came to the rescue, and extricated him from his perilous position. On another occasion a tremendous storm arose, lifting many of his boxes from the stall, breaking some glass squares he had for protection, and drifting his poems broadcast.

> There was such commotion, that he had a notion
> Old Satan was trying to plague him.

And yet amid all his discouragements, he has had very many things to cheer and encourage him. A young lady came to his stall one day and said, " There is one little book that you have written, entitled ' Uncle Peter,' which has been the means of reclaiming my only brother from a life of sin. He had begun to smoke and drink, and was rather gay; but since he has read that book, he has given up smoking and drinking, and is now an earnest Christian young man." This statement of course encouraged the Poet much, and he told her that such testimony was of more value than money, however necessary that might be for the purposes of life. Another young lady came and told him that this book had been the means of a young friend to whom she was engaged giving up smoking, and also the use of intoxicating drink ; and that he was coming personally to thank him for writing it, which he did some time after, and bringing for the Poet's inspection a beautiful silver watch, purchased with money saved since he had read " Uncle Peter," that would otherwise have been expended in smoke and drink. The Poet has also been personally thanked for writing this book by S. Morley, Esq., M.P., one of our nation's Christian philanthropists ; who recently sent the Poet a very kind letter, and also a cheque for three guineas ; stating that he regarded it but as a slight recognition for valuable life service. He also received by post, from some collegian, his opinion on this little book, to whom it had been sent evidently by some well-intentioned friend. This letter was not of so pleasing a character as the last, for from the Billingsgate language used in reference to the book, it was very evident that " Uncle Peter " had struck like an arrow in a sure place ; and had this unpromising young gentleman but have forwarded his address, the Poet would have replied to his disreputable communication ; and pointed out to him that, unless his future conduct became better than the language of his epistle, he might become some day a young man who would cause his father grief and his mother shame.

During the time the Poet has been pursuing his singular avocation, he has written hundreds of private pieces at the request of ladies and gentlemen—for friends' birthdays, wedding odes, and in memoriams, and many to try to heal differences among friends ; and he has done it in some cases with success. Many odes to lovers he has penned for both sexes, and never failed to give them in those odes what would be of real service, if through their life future it was faithfully carried out. Among the numerous communications received by post, there was one from a young lady in a distant county, intimiting that she understood the Clifton Poet could rule the planets, and she would be much obliged if he would forward her in the stamped envelope enclosed his charge for so doing, which she would remit, as she wanted to know her fate, and have her planet ruled. Such a request brought from the Poet a smile, and he wondered that there could be yet living in the world such fools as to believe that any living man could thus reveal the purposes of the Almighty. So, instead of sending for her money, and sending back a tissue of lies and nonsense, he forwarded her by return of post the following impromptu, which he trusts may be of service to others if there are yet living such credible beings :—

> The Clifton Poet writes Miss Fonce,
>   Not to let man befool her ;
> But send her wish to Heaven at once,
>   The only planet Ruler.

He never received a letter from this strange young lady for this good advice, which he felt was the best he could give her under the circumstances. The Poet at this time had been living more than two years alone since he had lost his daughter Mattie. It was for her sake that he had remained a widower for nearly twelve years, for they were happy together ; and he could never bear the thought of taking even a wife, and she again to leave him, and battle with the world, for she was not strong ; and if during her life he had done so, one of the conditions would have been that she should remain at home. An allwise Providence, however, removed her; and two years had fled since her decease. One of two courses was open to the Poet, for he had been living by himself until he felt it was no longer right ; and he must either take another wife, or dispose of his household goods and go to lodgings. This he did not think would add to his comfort, for he had always been happy in his married life in his own home ; aud he thought that the companionship of an affectionate wife would be better than sitting at ease, with no one to please ; and Providence provided one for him, younger than himself, 'tis true, but one that thoroughly understands him, and one that he thoroughly understands. Their marriage of few years' duration has hitherto been a happy one, for it seems to have given the Poet a new life, and something else to live for. They are blest with two little jewels—

> And Clifton, with all its abundance of wealth,
> Cannot purchase his jewels to-day.

Since their birth the poems on children have been written, and the Poet feels assured, in after years, that all right-minded persons will feel and say, that if the Poet's last marriage had only been the means of bringing out the children's poems, it would not have been in vain. A strange lady in London having seen in the *White Ribbon Army Gazette*—a Gospel Temperance periodical, in which many of the Clifton Poet's productions appear—a piece entitled "Watching Baby Sleep," wrote to him in reference to it, stating that she felt she must write ; and she was not ashamed to say while reading it she was *moved to tears*, and she thanked God there was one true Poet on the earth. The Poet smiled on reading this, and also felt assured there were many. Having, however, received such a pleasing acknowledgment from a lady, evidently a mother, induced him to insert these poems on children in this collection—although a very wealthy gentleman and an author questioned whether the poem, "Little Fingers," and some others, would be appreciated by the general public. The Poet heard him to the end, but has followed out his own convictions in publishing them for the following reasons : his friend who gave him this advice was a bachelor, and consequently not well qualified to judge in matters of this kind ; and further, the Poet feels that the children's poems will be welcome to many a father's and mother's heart. Soon after the Poet's last marriage, he was waited upon by the same meddlesome gentlemen on whom he wrote the impromptu, "Served him right;" who said, "I understand that you have had as many wives as there are fingers on my hand—one, two, three, four, five." "Then, sir," the Poet answered, "you are not the first gentleman who has been mistaken in reference to me. If it will be of any real service to you to know the truth, I will give it you. I have had four, and they have all been good ones."

> He turned aside, and went his way,
> Without another word to say :
> The Poet watched him down the hill,
> And wondered why he went so still.

Some years before this, while living at Keynsham, and with his third wife, he was accosted in the public street by one of those busybodies, who addressed him thus : " Why, sir, they tell me you have had three wives. Oh, dear ! " said he, " is it true ? " " I dare say it is," the Poet answered, " if it will be of any real service for you to know." " Why," he replied, " I never knew that before." " Did you not ? " said the Poet. " Well, you might have done if you had but have come to me and inquired. But I did not think it necessary, when I first came to Keynsham, to give the town crier a shilling to go through the streets and announce that I had the third good wife. If you should meet with anyone to whom the information will be useful, you will please let them know." A few years after this, when the Poet had been left a widower the third time, this same Mr. Officious came into the workshops where the Poet was foreman, and bawled out at the top of his voice, " I say, Mr. G., you should take to yourself another wife." The Poet looked straight at him, and said, " When I feel it right to take another wife, I shall do so, and not go paying clandestine visits to other people's wives." On hearing this he coloured to his temples, and bolted from the workshops as though he had been smitten in a sore place, followed by roaring peals of laughter from the workmen, who thought the Poet had heard a little of the doings of this meddlesome gentleman ; and I dare say they were right. These apparently trivial circumstances are referred to in the Poet's history only for the purpose of showing up these very meddlesome people, and teaching them if they are waiting and willing to be taught, that if they will but just look within themselves, they will find plenty of ways where they may more usefully be employed. While the Poet was living in Keynsham he wrote an acrostic on the Prince of Wales' recovery, entitled " Convalescence." He read it to the Rev. W. Pratt (Baptist Minister), who advised him to have it printed ; he thought it would be of service. This advice was carried out. It was printed in two colours ; and two of them were put in gilt frames, and forwarded to Windsor Castle, and graciously accepted by Her Majesty on behalf of herself and the Prince of Wales. Very many persons have at various times asked the Poet if he had not received many handsome presents from the important personages who had accepted his productions. He has not always satisfied the curiosity of such inquirers, when he felt they were fishing just for the purpose of wanting to know ; but he may venture here to make a frank and full confession, and the truthful answer is " No ! " And further, he never expected them, so he was never disappointed. His chief object in sending his writings to them was that they might see them, and if they could find time to read them, they would discover for what purpose they had been penned, namely, for doing good ; and that those who took an interest in pure literature—that which was calculated to make people true patriots, good citizens, and true Christians—might assist him in the circulation of his little books. A few have done this, but as yet comparatively very few indeed, the gentleman to whom this volume of poems is dedicated being an honourable exception. He has indeed been a true friend to the Poet, in many times sending for his publications, and giving them to Sunday Schools and bazaars gratuitously for distribution ; and he has done all this quietly and unobtrusively. And now the Poet deems it right to give honour to whom it is due ; and while he does this, he feels that there are many more in wealthy Clifton who might have done the same, and in doing it would have helped the Poet in doing good ; but with very few exceptions they have not done so. That was the reason his poem, " Dark Days," was published a short time ago, that those who were disposed might help him in his life's decline to toil on in a work that is far more important to humanity at large than all the exciting and unreal wonderments brought out on the stage. Some time ago, during the time that C. Thomas, Esq., was mayor of Bristol, the Poet had written a centenary poem for one of Bristol's native poets, R. Southey, Esq. He wrote this poem, which he considers his masterpiece, for two special reasons : first, because when he was a boy Southey's " Battle of Blenheim " poem made him a lover of peace, and to this day a denouncer of human butchery and hater of war ; and he feels to-day, that if all the clergy of the Church of England and ministers of dissenting congregations had but been faithful to their duty, in denouncing this blot on our boasted civilisation and caricature of the religion of the Lord Jesus Christ, this hateful and accursed thing would long ago have hidden its guilty head. His second reason for writing this poem, was because he loved Southey for his kindness to poor Henry Kirk White, when earthly friends were scarce, and his poor widowed mother, while he was sinking in a decline, felt the burden far too heavy for her purse to bear. The Poet sent a copy of this poem to C. Thomas, Esq., the then mayor, who sent him a very kind letter, expressing his admiration of the purity of its style, and begged the Poet's acceptance of the half-sovereign enclosed in the letter; and the present mayor, C. Wathen, Esq., on receipt of a few of the Poet's productions, forwarded him a kind complimentary letter from the mayoress and himself, and a donation of one pound. There are also a few ladies in Clifton who have been kind in having at different times a few of his little books, for the purpose of giving them to some who could not purchase them ; and while some few have done this, there are others who have been telling him for years that he is worthy of something better than being exposed to the winter's storms on Clifton Down, and yet they have never tried to lift him to that something, by helping him to circulate his books. By doing this they would have assisted him in doing good, and counteracting in some small degree the pernicious influence of what may be truly described as the silly fiction of the day ; and whatever tends to this must be one of the noblest pursuits of life : for a true Old Book declares that a man's life consisteth not in the abundance of the things which he possesseth in this world.

The Clifton Poet has often been requested to give answers to the following question : as to whether the life he had been pursuing during the last eleven years was not a very pleasant one? To this question he has to answer that there are two sides to it—at times it has been pleasant, at other times the reverse. Its pleasant side consists in feeling that you have done something to be appreciated by the sensible portion of mankind; and its unpleasant side is for a whole week to be exposed to the storms of St. Vincent's height, and his takings very often not exceeding five shillings per week, and sometimes not half of that. Take from this amount the cost of printing, and you will have for sum total what the Clifton Poet has often had, for writing pure literature in the midst of a wealthy people, who can give their money without stint to what neither benefits the bodies or souls of men. After this frank avowal, those who have considered the Clifton Poet to have had a lucrative occupation, will probably change their opinion. But the greatest trial the Poet ever had, while following his somewhat singular occupation, was this—and he feels he must relate it, for its recital may be of service to posterity, to teach them to act with more thought and Christian consistency than did those to whom it specially refers, should they ever be placed in similar circumstances. Some time ago a lecture was announced to be delivered in Colston Hall, by a minister in the city, entitled "Chatterton, the Poet Boy; or, a soul adrift." Of course there was, as is usual on such occasions, a large attendance to hear how the poor lad had gone adrift, and his very fearful end; and the Clifton Poet thought that night he would have a selection of his books there on a temporary stall, at the foot of the stairs, so that when the audience retired from the lecture they might have the opportunity of seeing the productions of one who was pursuing the same path, who was once a carpenter boy, and who had been connected with the Methodist family in church fellowship for nearly fifty years, and who for the twenty years he had resided in Bristol, had preached nearly as many sermons as any minister in it, and without any earthly remuneration. And he naturally concluded that from a Wesleyan audience he would at any rate get a small share of encouragement. But judge of his surprise. The whole company passed him by without any recognition, save a few solitary nods of the head. With one exception—a gentleman, Mark Whitwill, Esq., with his daughter had passed, when the Poet saw her whispering something in his ear, and he came back and said, "Let me have two of your books, please," and he left a shilling on the stall—twice the value of the books. But the Poet saw it not until after the gentleman had passed away, for his soul was too full of something else. He was thinking, "Yes; this is what sends poets' souls adrift—cold neglect. As it was in the days of Chatterton, so it is now, and apparently ever will be, world without end.

> Don't let them thrive—starve them alive—
>   Though they are toiling away :
> Then when they're dead, it can be said,
>   ' Oh, what a shame !   Lack a day !'"

And the reason may be given, because mankind generally prefer seeing their names emblazoned in the public papers on what they do, than quietly performing acts of Christian duty, in the way the Good Master recommended : " Let not thy right hand know what thy left hand doeth."   The Poet, feeling it to be his duty, sent an unvarnished statement of this evening's experiences to the minister who delivered this lecture, but it elicited from him no reply ; and, although he has passed the Poet's stall many times, he has never yet turned aside to give him a word of cheer—yet he knew, and well, that the Poet's productions were written for the purpose of leading people to that Saviour whom he professed to preach.   The Poet still thinks " What a wonderful age we live in ! " and he further wonders if there will be that kind of Spirit manifested in heaven !—if so, he is not particularly anxious to go until it is all banished.   He is just reminded, while writing down this incident, of another that deserves recording, that it may teach some would-be-thought pastors their simple duty as citizens, and especially as professing Christians.   One day, while the Poet was busy at his work in his little box—made with his own hands, to shelter him from the storm—two ministers, evidently of some Nonconformist Church, were taking note of the contents of the Poet's stall ; after remaining a short time, the Poet opened the door of his little sanctum and said, " Those books, gentlemen, are my own productions, if you will please examine them."   Without deigning to give even the respectful answer, " No, thank you," they somewhat haughtily turned aside, and walked away.   This touched a something within the Poet, that made him call out to the retiring reverends, " Will it be so in heaven ? "   This made them halt near the Poet's tree, and one of them called out, at the top of his voice, " No, it won't be so in heaven." " Then," said the Poet, " it has no right to be so on earth."   They then, without answering again, went on their way—with what reflections he knew not ; but his were, that such conduct would have been disreputable in a chimney-sweep, who had been respectfully addressed. And yet the Poet has not always had such reverend visitors: for he has had from many of the Church of England, and also Nonconformists, the greatest respect.   Some years ago, a clergyman, who has two livings in a distant county, came to see him ; and, on introducing himself, said, " Now I want to know, as briefly as you can give it, an account of your life-history, when and how you began verse writing, and whatever you can give me in that direction ; "—and then the two sat down, on that cold, January day, on a rustic seat near the Poet's stall.   The day before this the Poet had written there his lines on the author of " Home, sweet home," and he read them to this stranger, who said, " I should think you have never written anything like that before, have you ? " " Oh, yes," said the Poet, " and many ;   only I felt keenly while writing it, because it was the truth.   The author of ' Home, sweet home ' was homeless, and starving in a city, and heard a lady from her grand mansion sing his own sweet song.   And then, when he had been dead for thirty-two years,

> They took his poor bones
> From under the stones,

and shipped them off to America, at the request of the American Government, from Tunis, to have one of the grandest funerals ever witnessed in the United States."   Then the Poet gave this clergyman the details of his life-history, which appeared to greatly interest him ; and then he gave the Poet the substance of his own: which was that from once being a poor lad in the employ of Pickford & Co., at three shillings and sixpence per week, he had, by sheer plodding, and the blessing of Providence, worked himself up to his present position. Then with a hearty shake of the hand, some words of encouragement, and a something more—with a " Don't feel offended,"—they parted as true Christian friends: hoping to meet again, if not on earth, in heaven.   The Poet felt how different was the demeanour of this clergyman to one he had come in contact with on another occasion. He was a tall, severe looking specimen of humanity, appeared to be one of those strange characters, who could preach on the Sunday about the merciful Saviour of the world, and on Monday, whilst sitting on a magisterial bench, feel as though he would like to give some hungry looking wretch, who had been brought before him, three months' hard labour for looking through a hedge at a rabbit or hare sporting in the squire's grounds—not knowing or caring whether the poor fellow's family wanted food or not.   This strange clergyman made a dead halt before the Poet's stall, and said rather contemptuously " What have you got there ? " The Poet respectfully told him they were a few little books of his own writing. Then he exclaimed, " A strange kind of way this to get a living." " Is it, sir ? " said the Poet, " Does a man's life consist in the abundance of the things which he possesseth ?   My little books are written for doing good."   " If they are," said he, "why don't you ask the Lord Jesus to give you something better than this to get a living by ? " " What else better could I have," asked the Poet, " if I had but right encouragement ? Besides I am a great deal better off than the Lord Jesus ever was : I have food, raiment, friends to love me, and a comfortable home, and He had not where to lay His Head. He was despised and rejected of men, a man of sorrow and acquainted with grief—and would be again if He came into this world in the garb of poverty : for there are many persons to-day who would join the rabble multitude, and cry out : ' Crucify Him ! Crucify Him ! ' " and then looking at the clerical dignity, he exclaimed : " Ye know not what manner of spirit ye are of. There is many a peasant in a thatched cottage knows more to-day of the religion of Jesus Christ of the New Testament Scriptures, than some of those who are professing to be masters in Israel." Such are some of the varied life experiences of the Clifton Poet, living in the sixty-third year of his age, and from memory alone during the last few weeks have been committed to writing to accompany his " Heart Melodies for Storm and Sunshine." The number of incidents might have been increased, but he thinks that from what are here recorded, it will be quite evident to every attentive reader that his path as a poet has not been a smooth one ; and that the Poet who determines to battle with the evils of the age must prepare his mind for uphill work, and a great deal of it. Very many persons have made remarks in reference to the uncommon name of the Poet. He wishes to say in reference to this, that in the Counties of Nottingham and Lincoln there are many families who bear the same name ; and Mr. W. George, of the Book Stores, Park Street, Clifton, some time ago furnished him with the following, copied from an Old Bristol Directory, proving that in and near this city there were two families who had the same name : Gabbitass and Co., gunmakers, 1, King Street, 1775 ; and a Mrs. Mary Gabbitass, Shirehampton. The Clifton Poet feels he ought not to close this history of his life without referring to the great kindness and Christian friendliness manifested towards him by the Rev. W. Chapman, late Vicar of Christ Church, Clifton, who many times came to see him, and gave him words of cheer ; and also to the Rev. Arthur Hall, Congregational Minister, of Clifton Down, who, although a stranger to the Poet, came to see him, and by many kindly acts and words has shown that he understood the work of a Christian minister to one who, although not of the same church, was working for the same Master ; and with the hope cf meeting one day in the same sweet home, where there will be no high caste feeling to contend with ; but where all those who have usefully served their generation, by turning many to righteousness, will shine as the stars for ever and ever !

www.ingramcontent.com/pod-product-compliance
Lightning Source LLC
Chambersburg PA
CBHW081526040426
42447CB00013B/3357